THIS REPTILE CARE RECORD BOOK BELONGS TO

Edna Husted

Copyright © 2019 by CC Bearded Dragon Novelties.
All rights reserved. No part of this book may be used or reproduced in any manner whatsoever without written permission except in the case of brief quotations embodied in critical articles and interviews.

First edition: 2019

Insert Photo

PET INFO	
Name	
Breed	
Date of Birth	
Color	
Special Markings	
Allergies / Illnesses	
Behavior Info	
Feeding Instructions	
Other Notes	

march 29 2021

Insert Photo

PET INFO

Name	Micheal
Breed	dk
Date of Birth	June 15
Color	yellow purple
Special Markings	slightly amputated tail
Allergies / Illnesses	none that Ik of
Behavior Info	Lazy
Feeding Instructions	fave food carrots blubarys
Other Notes	

Insert Photo

PET INFO	
Name	
Breed	
Date of Birth	
Color	
Special Markings	
Allergies / Illnesses	
Behavior Info	
Feeding Instructions	
Other Notes	

Insert Photo

PET INFO	
Name	
Breed	
Date of Birth	
Color	
Special Markings	
Allergies / Illnesses	
Behavior Info	
Feeding Instructions	
Other Notes	

Insert Photo

PET INFO	
Name	
Breed	
Date of Birth	
Color	
Special Markings	
Allergies / Illnesses	
Behavior Info	
Feeding Instructions	
Other Notes	

Insert Photo

PET INFO	
Name	
Breed	
Date of Birth	
Color	
Special Markings	
Allergies / Illnesses	
Behavior Info	
Feeding Instructions	
Other Notes	

Notes

Daily Care Log

Date: mon 29 2021

FEEDINGS

Pet	Food	Total	Finished
Micheal	letuce, cricket poweder		

CLEANINGS

Pet	BM/Urine	Bath Time
Mick	1	

ADDITIONAL RECORD & REMINDER

April 2,@@	give bath wed

Notes

Daily Care Log

Date : _____

FEEDINGS			
Pet	Food	Total	Finished

CLEANINGS		
Pet	BM/Urine	Bath Time

ADDITIONAL RECORD & REMINDER	

Notes

Daily Care Log

Date : _____

FEEDINGS

Pet	Food	Total	Finished

CLEANINGS

Pet	BM/Urine	Bath Time

ADDITIONAL RECORD & REMINDER

Notes

Daily Care Log

Date : _____

FEEDINGS			
Pet	Food	Total	Finished

CLEANINGS		
Pet	BM/Urine	Bath Time

ADDITIONAL RECORD & REMINDER	

Notes

Daily Care Log

Date : _____

	FEEDINGS		
Pet	Food	Total	Finished

	CLEANINGS	
Pet	BM/Urine	Bath Time

ADDITIONAL RECORD & REMINDER	

Notes

Daily Care Log

Date: _____

FEEDINGS			
Pet	Food	Total	Finished

CLEANINGS		
Pet	BM/Urine	Bath Time

ADDITIONAL RECORD & REMINDER	

Notes

Daily Care Log

Date : _____

FEEDINGS

Pet	Food	Total	Finished

CLEANINGS

Pet	BM/Urine	Bath Time

ADDITIONAL RECORD & REMINDER

Notes

Daily Care Log

Date : _____

FEEDINGS			
Pet	Food	Total	Finished

CLEANINGS		
Pet	BM/Urine	Bath Time

ADDITIONAL RECORD & REMINDER	

Notes

Daily Care Log

Date : _____

FEEDINGS

Pet	Food	Total	Finished

CLEANINGS

Pet	BM/Urine	Bath Time

ADDITIONAL RECORD & REMINDER

Notes

Daily Care Log

Date : _____

FEEDINGS

Pet	Food	Total	Finished

CLEANINGS

Pet	BM/Urine	Bath Time

ADDITIONAL RECORD & REMINDER

Notes

Daily Care Log

Date : _____

FEEDINGS

Pet	Food	Total	Finished

CLEANINGS

Pet	BM/Urine	Bath Time

ADDITIONAL RECORD & REMINDER

Notes

Daily Care Log

Date : _____

FEEDINGS

Pet	Food	Total	Finished

CLEANINGS

Pet	BM/Urine	Bath Time

ADDITIONAL RECORD & REMINDER

Notes

Daily Care Log

Date : _____

FEEDINGS

Pet	Food	Total	Finished

CLEANINGS

Pet	BM/Urine	Bath Time

ADDITIONAL RECORD & REMINDER

Notes

Daily Care Log

Date : _____

FEEDINGS

Pet	Food	Total	Finished

CLEANINGS

Pet	BM/Urine	Bath Time

ADDITIONAL RECORD & REMINDER

Notes

Daily Care Log

Date : _____

FEEDINGS			
Pet	Food	Total	Finished

CLEANINGS		
Pet	BM/Urine	Bath Time

ADDITIONAL RECORD & REMINDER	

Notes

Daily Care Log

Date : _____

FEEDINGS

Pet	Food	Total	Finished

CLEANINGS

Pet	BM/Urine	Bath Time

ADDITIONAL RECORD & REMINDER

Notes

Daily Care Log

Date : _____

FEEDINGS			
Pet	Food	Total	Finished

CLEANINGS		
Pet	BM/Urine	Bath Time

ADDITIONAL RECORD & REMINDER	

Notes

Daily Care Log

Date : _____

FEEDINGS

Pet	Food	Total	Finished

CLEANINGS

Pet	BM/Urine	Bath Time

ADDITIONAL RECORD & REMINDER

Notes

Daily Care Log

Date : _____

FEEDINGS			
Pet	Food	Total	Finished

CLEANINGS		
Pet	BM/Urine	Bath Time

ADDITIONAL RECORD & REMINDER	

Notes

Daily Care Log

Date : _____

FEEDINGS			
Pet	Food	Total	Finished

CLEANINGS		
Pet	BM/Urine	Bath Time

ADDITIONAL RECORD & REMINDER	

Notes

Daily Care Log

Date : _____

FEEDINGS

Pet	Food	Total	Finished

CLEANINGS

Pet	BM/Urine	Bath Time

ADDITIONAL RECORD & REMINDER

Notes

Daily Care Log

Date : _____

FEEDINGS			
Pet	Food	Total	Finished

CLEANINGS		
Pet	BM/Urine	Bath Time

ADDITIONAL RECORD & REMINDER	

Notes

Daily Care Log   Date : _____

FEEDINGS			
Pet	Food	Total	Finished

CLEANINGS		
Pet	BM/Urine	Bath Time

ADDITIONAL RECORD & REMINDER	

Notes

Daily Care Log

Date : _____

FEEDINGS

Pet	Food	Total	Finished

CLEANINGS

Pet	BM/Urine	Bath Time

ADDITIONAL RECORD & REMINDER

Notes

Daily Care Log

Date : _____

FEEDINGS

Pet	Food	Total	Finished

CLEANINGS

Pet	BM/Urine	Bath Time

ADDITIONAL RECORD & REMINDER

Notes

Daily Care Log

Date : _____

FEEDINGS

Pet	Food	Total	Finished

CLEANINGS

Pet	BM/Urine	Bath Time

ADDITIONAL RECORD & REMINDER

Notes

Daily Care Log

Date : _____

FEEDINGS			
Pet	Food	Total	Finished

CLEANINGS		
Pet	BM/Urine	Bath Time

ADDITIONAL RECORD & REMINDER	

Notes

Daily Care Log

Date : _____

FEEDINGS

Pet	Food	Total	Finished

CLEANINGS

Pet	BM/Urine	Bath Time

ADDITIONAL RECORD & REMINDER

Notes

Daily Care Log

Date : _____

FEEDINGS

Pet	Food	Total	Finished

CLEANINGS

Pet	BM/Urine	Bath Time

ADDITIONAL RECORD & REMINDER

Notes

Daily Care Log

Date : _____

FEEDINGS

Pet	Food	Total	Finished

CLEANINGS

Pet	BM/Urine	Bath Time

ADDITIONAL RECORD & REMINDER

Notes

Daily Care Log   Date : _____

FEEDINGS

Pet	Food	Total	Finished

CLEANINGS

Pet	BM/Urine	Bath Time

ADDITIONAL RECORD & REMINDER

Notes

Daily Care Log

Date : _____

FEEDINGS

Pet	Food	Total	Finished

CLEANINGS

Pet	BM/Urine	Bath Time

ADDITIONAL RECORD & REMINDER

Notes

Daily Care Log

Date : _____

FEEDINGS

Pet	Food	Total	Finished

CLEANINGS

Pet	BM/Urine	Bath Time

ADDITIONAL RECORD & REMINDER

Notes

Daily Care Log

Date : _____

FEEDINGS

Pet	Food	Total	Finished

CLEANINGS

Pet	BM/Urine	Bath Time

ADDITIONAL RECORD & REMINDER

Notes

Daily Care Log

Date : _____

FEEDINGS

Pet	Food	Total	Finished

CLEANINGS

Pet	BM/Urine	Bath Time

ADDITIONAL RECORD & REMINDER

Notes

Daily Care Log

Date : _____

FEEDINGS

Pet	Food	Total	Finished

CLEANINGS

Pet	BM/Urine	Bath Time

ADDITIONAL RECORD & REMINDER

Notes

Daily Care Log

Date : _____

FEEDINGS			
Pet	Food	Total	Finished

CLEANINGS		
Pet	BM/Urine	Bath Time

ADDITIONAL RECORD & REMINDER	

Notes

Daily Care Log

Date : _____

FEEDINGS

Pet	Food	Total	Finished

CLEANINGS

Pet	BM/Urine	Bath Time

ADDITIONAL RECORD & REMINDER

Notes

Daily Care Log

Date : _____

FEEDINGS

Pet	Food	Total	Finished

CLEANINGS

Pet	BM/Urine	Bath Time

ADDITIONAL RECORD & REMINDER

Notes

Daily Care Log

Date : _____

FEEDINGS

Pet	Food	Total	Finished

CLEANINGS

Pet	BM/Urine	Bath Time

ADDITIONAL RECORD & REMINDER

Notes

Daily Care Log

Date : _____

FEEDINGS

Pet	Food	Total	Finished

CLEANINGS

Pet	BM/Urine	Bath Time

ADDITIONAL RECORD & REMINDER

Notes

Daily Care Log

Date : _____

FEEDINGS

Pet	Food	Total	Finished

CLEANINGS

Pet	BM/Urine	Bath Time

ADDITIONAL RECORD & REMINDER

Notes

Daily Care Log

Date : _____

FEEDINGS

Pet	Food	Total	Finished

CLEANINGS

Pet	BM/Urine	Bath Time

ADDITIONAL RECORD & REMINDER

Notes

Daily Care Log

Date : _____

FEEDINGS

Pet	Food	Total	Finished

CLEANINGS

Pet	BM/Urine	Bath Time

ADDITIONAL RECORD & REMINDER

Notes

Daily Care Log

Date : _____

FEEDINGS			
Pet	Food	Total	Finished

CLEANINGS		
Pet	BM/Urine	Bath Time

ADDITIONAL RECORD & REMINDER	

Notes

Daily Care Log

Date : _____

FEEDINGS

Pet	Food	Total	Finished

CLEANINGS

Pet	BM/Urine	Bath Time

ADDITIONAL RECORD & REMINDER

Notes

Daily Care Log

Date : _____

FEEDINGS

Pet	Food	Total	Finished

CLEANINGS

Pet	BM/Urine	Bath Time

ADDITIONAL RECORD & REMINDER

Notes

Daily Care Log

Date : _____

FEEDINGS

Pet	Food	Total	Finished

CLEANINGS

Pet	BM/Urine	Bath Time

ADDITIONAL RECORD & REMINDER

Notes

Daily Care Log

Date : _____

FEEDINGS			
Pet	Food	Total	Finished

CLEANINGS		
Pet	BM/Urine	Bath Time

ADDITIONAL RECORD & REMINDER	

Notes

Daily Care Log

Date : _____

FEEDINGS

Pet	Food	Total	Finished

CLEANINGS

Pet	BM/Urine	Bath Time

ADDITIONAL RECORD & REMINDER

Notes

Daily Care Log

Date : _____

FEEDINGS			
Pet	Food	Total	Finished

CLEANINGS		
Pet	BM/Urine	Bath Time

ADDITIONAL RECORD & REMINDER	

Notes

Daily Care Log

Date : _____

FEEDINGS			
Pet	Food	Total	Finished

CLEANINGS		
Pet	BM/Urine	Bath Time

ADDITIONAL RECORD & REMINDER	

Notes

Daily Care Log

Date : _____

FEEDINGS			
Pet	Food	Total	Finished

CLEANINGS		
Pet	BM/Urine	Bath Time

ADDITIONAL RECORD & REMINDER	

Notes

Daily Care Log

Date : _____

FEEDINGS

Pet	Food	Total	Finished

CLEANINGS

Pet	BM/Urine	Bath Time

ADDITIONAL RECORD & REMINDER

Notes

Daily Care Log

Date : _____

FEEDINGS

Pet	Food	Total	Finished

CLEANINGS

Pet	BM/Urine	Bath Time

ADDITIONAL RECORD & REMINDER

Notes

Daily Care Log

Date : _____

FEEDINGS

Pet	Food	Total	Finished

CLEANINGS

Pet	BM/Urine	Bath Time

ADDITIONAL RECORD & REMINDER

Notes

Made in the USA
Columbia, SC
11 March 2021